Our Delicate Barricades Downed

Other Books by William Reichard

The Night Horse: New and Selected Poems (Brighthorse Books, 2018)

Two Men Rowing Madly Toward Infinity (Broadstone Books, 2016)

As Breath in Winter (MIEL Press, 2015)

American Tensions: Literature of Identity and the Search for Social Justice
(New Village Press, 2011)

Sin Eater (Mid-List Press, 2010)

This Brightness (Mid-List Press, 2007)

How To (Mid-List Press, 2004)

The Evening Crowd at Kirmser's: A Gay Life in the 1940's
(University of Minnesota Press, 2001)

An Alchemy in the Bones (New Rivers Press, 1999)

Our Delicate Barricades Downed

Prose Poems

William Reichard

Broadstone

Library of Congress Control No. 2020950296
ISBN 978-1-937968-75-5

Text and cover design by Larry W. Moore
Cover cyanotype by the author

Broadstone Books
An Imprint of
Broadstone Media LLC
418 Ann Street
Frankfort, KY 40601-1929
BroadstoneBooks.com

CONTENTS

Two Horses

The pasture, like the road, dips and swells. The sky stains all it touches yellow-pink. The air is too cool, but I have the windows down, and I'm surrounded by the rich scent of fresh mown fields. An ancient oak forest abuts a freeway wall, a chain store, then a barn. In a rolling meadow, two brown horses glow in the morning's light. They run toward me, then turn away, pulling the last of the dark into the day.

A LOST BOY

Listen: the wind whispers through the tall corn. Gather the syllables together as you walk each row. Hold your hands up to hold the leaves' sharp edges away from your soft face. No caresses here. Only cutting. One row to the next. Collect the sounds. String them together in the milky moonlight until words are formed. You knew how to listen to them once, could comprehend the land's language, but you've been away too long. All of the green has flowed out of your veins. You cannot translate the language of this quiet country.

Poor

The shuttered bar's wall collapses, falls into the Laundromat. Dirty clothes for days and nowhere to wash the oversized blankets, the heavy quilts stitched from remnants of Grandmother's dresses. Winter is coming so they get out the lath and heavy plastic. I knew families who lived like that, broken windows patched with canvas tarps, frozen breath forming clouds in the unheated kitchen. I knew families who depended on the meat their men would hunt each autumn. No game meant nothing to eat, shame-faced trips to the food shelves. A semblance of strength trumped the cries of a hungry child, and I would see those kids in the school hallways, pale and thin, lacking breakfast and focus. I was one of those kids, could always spot my kind, missing dead fathers, mothers eaten up by poor pay at local factories. Someone might ask: *how poor are you?* But you could not say, not to teachers, not to friends. Silence equaled strength, the ability to deny yourself everything. Those houses are empty now, bankrupt or abandoned, farmsteads unable to support any family. I see them on my way to visit my elderly mother. The animals take over, and trees grow up through kitchen floors. Upper bedrooms become aviaries, full of birds and owls that eat the birds, with bats sequestered in every corner.

Disappearing into the Trees

When I was a child, I never thought about my body, she said, sitting across from me in the tea shop, sipping Lapsang Souchong, savoring its heavy, wood smoked scent. Now she has two plastic knees, her arthritic fingers cramp painfully in the cold, and she lives daily with her body's tyranny.

It wasn't the same for me. I didn't have the luxury of not thinking about my body. I always did. I was such a skinny child. My ribs and shoulder blades stuck out like small backward wings whenever I tucked in my shirt. My sternum was concave, my arms too thin. I thought, growing up, that my body was wrong. Something shifted in my mother's womb before my birth. My body was proof of this.

In order for me to believe I was born in the wrong body, I needed to be trained. Television taught me. Drive-in movies taught me. Mr. Brady, of *The Brady Bunch*, playing a man who became a woman on an episode of *Medical Center*, taught me; poor Robert Reed, closeted and afraid, dying of AIDS all those years later, taught me. And Rock Hudson. And Liberace. And Freddie Mercury. Literature taught me. And magazines. Billboards, pop music, family stories. All of these, such good teachers.

When I was a child, I hid in the trees, I told her, sipping my tea, staring out the plate glass shop front at the sugar maples lining the boulevard. They were burning red, every one, the way they must, when winter is only a breath away.

When I was a child, I'd hide in the rhubarb patch, I said, *those giant leaves big enough to cover a ten-year-old's body.* I loved the trees in the yard of the house I grew up in: burr oak, silver maple, birch, elm. I trusted the trees to stand between me and the world. I trusted them not to fall.

Night

It was dark on the country roads, and the moon was slight, a small crescent in the sky. The stars were white clusters shining backward through time, mere ghosts of light.

When I drove over the wooden bridge that spanned the river where I learned to swim, I stopped, shut off the engine, and sat. I felt the weight of summer air, not heavy, exactly, but fair, an almost liquid mix, thick, like I could grab handfuls of it and hurl it, in slow motion, across space. I heard crickets, and water's constant chatter. I heard the crisp, brittle footfalls of animals in the nearby forest, the wind in summer leaves. This was the way my whole childhood had been: ears not yet closed to the way the unseen world spoke, finally, out loud in the darkness.

A Question of the Body

The soil there was primarily clay, sticky, slick. Harvesting carrots, radishes, beets, washing the clinging dirt away with icy well water. And the water, full of iron. So strong a single glass left the taste of metal in my mouth. Yet it didn't steel me against that hard life. The air there was filled with conflicting scents: fresh mown alfalfa against the stench of the stockyard next door; peony and piss; lilac and tractor exhaust. My blood was iron. My blood was smoke from the endless stream of cigarettes my family consumed. Cut me and a whisp of burnt tobacco drifted from the wound. My bones were trees: oak, silver maple, ash, boxelder. My hair, the weightless fluff from the cottonwood's seeds. My body, the flat land, the subtle hills that rolled from acre to acre. Frigid river water, the unseen undercurrent, the brackish pools near the shore, my nerves, spreading out in endless tributaries. What held me together: gravel roads and hot tar, snowdrifts and icicles, sheer will, dreams, confusion.

SOMETHING FOR WHICH THERE IS NO WORD

The thin white muslin curtains flutter in an early spring breeze. How odd our language is, that we can say cloth moves in the manner of a butterfly's wings. But there is no better word. Perhaps in another language.

In a Bergman film, whose plot I've forgotten, there are moments in between moments, scenes in between scenes. Soft light on a bowl of fruit sitting on a well-worn wooden table. The color of a weathered bench near a stout back door. The evanescent quality of shadows on summer nights that are as bright as day.

Needlepoint

Imagine the world stitched, like the Bayeux Tapestry. Each day a set of threads and knots, intricate, incredible in color and design, absolutely accurate. Given a needle and a pair of shears, which days would you prick and clip until they were indecipherable, a mass of tangled threads hanging down, unable to relate any story? What tiny betrayals would you unweave from history? The old dog's death? Drain cleaner in the instant coffee? The tricycle thrown at your sister's head? Your father's sad life and ignoble death? Given a needle and a few spools of thread, which days might you sew back, minus the sorrow, minus the pain that gives birth to regret?

Haunted House Hunting

The bent, rusted hinges and frayed wood of the frame prove that once, this house had a door. Now it's open to the world. The outside lives inside. As we walk into the ancient kitchen, we test the floor. No one wants to fall through to the basement. We didn't bring flashlights, and though the moon is full, it doesn't shine bright enough to illuminate each dark room. My brother-in-law finds a large plastic doll on a rusty bedframe. He sets its hair on fire, then holds the doll up by one leg. She's a gruesome torch. For as long as I can remember, we've sought out these abandoned houses, long empty, full of decay. They usually stand in small wooded lots, completely encased by corn or soybean fields, with narrow, rutted paths the only route in or out. We only explore them at night. We're not searching for anything tangible, no antiques or fancy woodwork to salvage. If anyone asked us why we do this, and why in the dark, we'd struggle to articulate the reason. Because the darkness is soft. Because it makes allowances for old fears and faults. We don't want ghosts. We know they're here, but we're blind to them, gratefully so.

Seven Sisters

Most of them married drunks because their mother married a drunk; it was almost a tradition. Mean men with bad jobs or no jobs who got even meaner when they drank, and they drank every day. They lived in ramshackle old houses on untended farms, or on the outskirts of identical small towns, where the noise they made wouldn't bother the neighbors. One lived in a trailer house perched on the edge of a working gravel pit. Her husband was a night guard there. Each sister suffered the predictable beatings. Some of them carried the bruises defiantly, even proudly, as if to proclaim, *this is how much I love my man*. Others hid them under long-sleeved shirts, even in summer. Those stunted, red-nosed men with bloodshot eyes and rough hands always wanted to fight. Most of the sisters stayed and hoped for change or death. One left. The rest hated her for it.

THE FIRST MAN

He'd been the mayor for thirty years, town veterinarian, mentor of fatherless boys. He took them along on house calls to isolated farms to treat sick cattle, injured dogs. Or drove them to town to buy their first suits for prom or graduation. After the sheriff found him dead, the top of his head opened up to the sky, shotgun still in his hands, each secret he thought he'd kept began to speak. How many had there been? Whose sons were so ashamed of what he'd done to them, they could never speak it, had buried it so deep it finally spilled out in closed fists, stolen prescriptions? A good town knows how to silence its own. The residents willed themselves to forget. Still, he'd named each street in the new subdivision after his children.

ABANDONED SAWMILLS

There were only ruins by the time I came along. Crumbling brick walls dug into the hillsides near the railroad tracks. Rough stone floors. The only artifacts were pieces of broken pottery and rusty hunks of metal whose purpose was lost to time. This is where all of the trees had gone, those that must have grown in the spaces now plowed into flat fields. The stories I heard were numerous, but always repeated a common theme: a sawmill, an accident, a man who lost the top of his head to a hungry, trunk-splitting blade. In one version, he was the father of someone I barely knew, whose name I recognized. I dug furiously into those hillsides, hoping to find the top of that man's skull, worn smooth with age, now resembling a shallow gray cup. I had the idea that if I drank from that gruesome vessel, something would change. I would change. I would be made better.

GENIUS/CRAZY

Everyone said, if you're too smart, you'll go crazy. He was highly intelligent. Six foot six and three hundred pounds. His mind was a dazzling maze that none of his teachers could comprehend. A kind word from a girl three classes below him was misconstrued, triggered a keen awareness of his own desperate loneliness. He thought he loved her. He heard God's voice in his head, telling him he and the girl were spiritually wed. She didn't know his name. He sent her endless rambling letters full of brilliance and threat. He mentioned a body found near her home a few months before. He mentioned the inevitability of heaven. They took him to the state hospital when someone spotted him lying on a picnic table next to the granite memorial to the war dead, masturbating, in the small park in the center of town. The townspeople looked away as the ambulance disappeared down the two-lane blacktop. He became the stuff of whispers. The girl forgot him.

Round Hay Bales

Delicately curling in upon themselves, as a galaxy curls in upon itself: Containment. Infinity. Our ruins. The closest we will ever come to an Acropolis or a Pompeii. They stand singly, sometimes in pairs or in groups, dropped where the farmers left them when winter forced everyone inside. Broken columns—home to small lives—mice, squirrels—they sag under the snow's weight, begin to lean, to rot, to return to the soil from which they sprang.

Town Florist

His claim to fame was the doll hanging in the attic window of the house he grew up in. It was featured in national guidebooks on weird byways: *the Janesville Doll*. He knew who put it there, and why, but would never say. That mystery was his currency. He did all of the local weddings and funerals. Everyone admired his work, so sculptural and elegant, just this side of spare. After his mother died, he lived on in that notorious house. He didn't socialize, as far as anyone knew, and what he did when he wasn't arranging flowers, no one said. Privacy can be valued more than gossip in some small towns, because everyone you know has some dirt on you, and you on them. Such a silent, polite détente.

RUINED BARN

The crumbling ramp is covered in grass, and the barn's roof bears a thick coat of moss; it's startling, that green against summer's sharp blue sky. The walls are weathered: red turned silver-gray where the paint has faded or peeled. I saw this barn for the first time when I drove past it on my way to a new life in college. I had just turned eighteen. Then, I found it sad, a sagging reminder of all I thought I was leaving behind. Now, I see its beauty, what great damage time has heaped upon it, and find it more beautiful for all of its flaws.

Prairie Crossing

Nights, we shared the sleeper, taking turns because of space: my father and me; my brother and me; my father and my brother. The odd man out got the passenger seat. No one slept. Our father was used to traveling alone, and my brother and I were too young to spend three weeks in a semi with the old man.

The prairie churned along, the wheat like waves in a dry, golden sea, the three of us swimming through heat, through asphalt, through the emptiness of Iowa, North Dakota, Minnesota—every flat state.

Lunch and dinner at truck stops, some with showers, none were clean. Progression of malts, fries, and burgers until we had to pull over on an empty road in the Badlands so I could throw up on the edge of that vast, painted desert.

All I could see was the highway, the houses whose components we delivered, the workmen waiting at the building sites for whole rooms unloaded from our truck. All I could think of was what was behind me: my mother; summer gardens; good books; my own bed; no roads leading anywhere but home.

In the Shoulder Season

Light rain weaves a damp net over my body, a clinging shawl. Fog is born in the collision between one season and another, and it has the power to render me invisible. I walk between thick and thin pockets of it, appearing only from streetlight to streetlight, now here, now gone. The rain is so fine tonight that I cannot call it rain. Instead: misty silk organza; god's wet breath.

PASTORAL

What passes here for picturesque begins, always, with a field and
ends with an isolated stand of trees, a dwindling stream, or the
sharp interruption of a small town cut into the green landscape.
No matter how far you travel away from this place, the flatness
stays with you, the expectation that every mountain will end in
a smooth plateau, flat stacked upon flat, impossibly rising up to
the sky. When I was a boy I'd ride my bike for hours, speeding
down rough gravel roads that always formed great grids filled with
fields and the occasional farmstead, their gravel drives a mile long
stretching from the road to the house. We all liked our privacy. But
gossip has wings, and flies fast along telephone wires, or simply
drifts on the wind, carrying unheralded though not unwelcomed
news from one ear to the next.

Polar Vortex

Endless white. Trees shrouded in hoar frost. The streets and side-walks, ice white. Cars transformed into huge white mounds, tires frozen to the road. The landscape reduced to a few shades of white, and the horizon, vanished, sandwiched between white land, white sky. It is all so brittle. The slightest pressure and it will shatter. The birds that overwinter are frozen in the trees and drop, solid, to the ground, dusted white in their cold shrouds. Footprints vanish in the bitter snow. The only sound: white wind. Such numb continuity, such white monotony in these dizzy, frigid spells that grow longer each year. I open the front door to get the morning paper and my breath is captured by the cold, becomes a solid white cloud, and floats away.

THE MAN IN THE RED SHIRT

Here lies a boy who has a dream. The same dream every night. The same dream for over a year. He's just beginning to fall asleep when a cloud coalesces in the pooling moonlight. It resembles the Milky Way, a swirl of bright particles that grows into the shape of a man. Every night, the same dream. The man's hair and beard are black, he wears a blood-red shirt, and his eyes are too luminous, his skin too white, his face, a mask of malice. When the boy tries to move, his muscles are lax. When he tries to scream, his voice has vanished. The man moves slowly toward the bed. The boy is trapped in his body. *I'm going to kill you*, he hears the man say, though his lips don't move, and he floats, more than walks, till he stands directly over the boy. He places his hands around the boy's throat and begins to squeeze. The boy sees the stars that shape the man's body, each an orb that has its own face. He blacks out. He tells his family what happens each night, the same dream, and they shrug or laugh or assume it's a lie. Who listens to the dreams of children? Who pays attention to their wild imaginations? Every day must fall into darkness. Every star in the sky must shine. Poor child in the night. The moonlight is merciless. His screams are emptied into the dark.

WINTER GARDEN *(GHOST STORY I)*

I knew she would want irises in winter. My sister wasn't a contrary
woman, she was always hungry for the things the world denies us.
She asked me, on her deathbed, to help our family reconcile with
the dead, and then died, leaving the rest of us to make our uneasy
alliances. I felt bitter about it then, the peace she asked all of us to
find, then found herself in a place where, I suspect, dreams could
no longer trouble her.

A friend came to visit my family, and later said, *your family lives
with the dead*. He said he could see them standing there, hear their
voices as clearly as those who survived. He added that the evolution
of the soul demands, at best, reconciliation; at least, ease, a way of
going on living with the dead, not in spite of them.

Each January first, her birthday, I buy a dozen irises, and drive to
a bridge that spans the icy Mississippi. One by one, I throw the
flowers in. Their deep purple is too vivid against winter's awful
gray. I do this thing for her, but nothing else. We all have to find
what comfort we can. I let the water carry my gift to wherever it
is she has found to call heaven.

WE LUTHERANS

Polished deep into the pale blonde pews, polished deep into the plain wooden cross on the altar of austerity, in the sanctuary of silence where only the pastor ever spoke in words above a whisper, every breath, cough, sneeze, or rustle of tissue-thin hymnal pages was heard and commented on later by the ladies who served lunch in the basement after service. Such plainness in the architecture, as if God would grow angry at any hint of the ostentatious. We couldn't find God in a house too holy for anyone not born in or related to anyone else in the area. We lost our faith listening to the whispered laughter of our neighbors, who found humor in the holes in the soles of someone's shoes, made visible when she knelt to take communion. Between the modulating notes of the tone-deaf soprano and the stern sermons against desire, there was no space to breathe. Between moderation in every action and modesty implicitly demanded, there was no life. In the brown pews and the unadorned altar, in the invisible Christ on the pure blonde cross, I grew distrustful. Life, in our town, seemed to be lived in the darker corners, away from the light from the pebbleglass windows, in the looks the neighbors gave because our family's "anonymous" donation envelope didn't sound heavy enough when our mother dropped it into the tarnished silver collection bowl each Sunday.

Long Gravel Drive

There was nothing special about that place. Local teenagers, on drunken weekend nights, used to dare each other to travel down the lonely gravel drive, pull up to the long-abandoned house, and go inside. Something inhabited that house. Call it a ghost or call it a memory, an event so vivid it was etched into the lath and plaster walls. In the presence of a living soul, the thing played itself out, like a record with a scratch, so every time the music started, it would play up to one exact moment, then jump back to the beginning again. Over and over, a dark form, an arm raised, a scream, a hammer blow. The whole family dead and the murderer never found. If you went in, you didn't stay long, and after you ran out, nearly paralyzed by fear, you lied to your friends, told them it was nothing, called them chicken shits when they wouldn't take their turn inside.

Country Queers *(Long Ago)*

There were many who never married; those out hiding in the cornfields; those out walking in the trees. There were many who said they hadn't met the right one yet; who lived with their mothers until their mothers died; many who lived, then, having run out of excuses. There were bachelor farmers born out of a long tradition of men who lived for their land. There were women who cleaned the church pews; those who cooked for the priest; those so devout they might as well have been nuns. There were the brothers who were not brothers; sisters who were not sisters; those who didn't socialize; those who wouldn't mix; those who never opened their mouths, those who married silence. There were those who did marry and those who had children; those who crept from the family bed and found what they needed at wayside rests; those who never married but had one roommate for life. There were those who cut themselves off from family; those whose families cut them off. There were those who disappeared, suitcase in hand; those who disappeared but took nothing with them. There were those who chose a quiet death; those who wed the river; those who wed the rope. There were those who waited. There were those who spoke. There were those who lived; those who lived and thrived.

Country Love Song

The two sides of his face didn't match after the car accident, and there was a slight indentation near the back of his skull, where they'd had to remove bone when his brain swelled. He was a kind man, and he loved my sister, who was already sick with the disease that would later kill her. Some called him slow. Maybe he was. He worked on his family's hog farm a couple of counties over. He didn't always understand jokes, and his speech was very considered. He used the archaic past tense of eat whenever our mother invited him to dinner. *No thank you. I already et.* He asked my sister to marry him, but she declined. I never understood why. Kind men are rare. A few years later, my sister died, and one day, I heard that he had passed. Another car accident. He'd been speeding down the country road he grew up on. He knew every inch of that gravel track. As he reached the top of a small hill, he met another car. There was a head-on collision. What he never knew: the other driver was his own brother. Both men died.

Unexplained Death

Sunlight, filtered through a liquid lens, ripples as it reaches toward the lake's bottom. In winter, it cannot reach the lake's silt floor. He was in the truck when they found him. His eyes open, as if looking out through the water, searching for every other lost thing that rested where he rested. Not a heart attack, the officials said, not alcohol or drugs, no medical condition. No one will say *suicide* in a small town. It could cause decades of talk, and his family wanted him buried in the Catholic cemetery, next to his son, who'd died of AIDS (though they called it cancer) over twenty years before. He was simply dead. Having lived his whole life in that place, he knew where the aeration system sat at the bottom of the lake; the system's pump kept ice from sealing the water's surface in winter, so the fish wouldn't suffocate. That's where the police found him a few days after he went missing, his body gently rocking in the icy water.

CURTAIN OF RAIN

Standing at the edge of a field in summer, I see it: a wall cloud. It bears an air of architectural grandeur. The air fills with the scent of rain before rain begins, and the sun shines almost brilliantly, a last great blaze before it's lost in the churning gray. Daylight fades. The rain's wall moves so swiftly. Quick! Into the old barn's doorway! The curtain of rain crosses the yard and I witness that moment when it moves right over me, bifurcating the world into all that's wet, and all that's dry.

In Dreams

The darkness is pitiless. I can't sleep through the night, so spend hours in a perpetual twilight, as in those towns in the far north, where, in winter, it's never daylight, only a slow arc between dusk and darkness. Sleep comes fitfully, from my body's primordial fear that, in too long a rest, my soul might take flight and never find its way home. The ancient Egyptians called this the *Ka*, the soul that, nightly, left the body asleep and soared out across the sky.

In the final dream I had about my sister, I was sitting in the kitchen of our childhood home. The phone rang. I answered. It was her. She was calling from beyond. It was a poor connection. Her voice was almost unintelligable amidst crackling static and the cries of desperate others who also wanted contact. It was a short conversation. She wanted to say goodbye because *they* wouldn't allow her to call again. *Who are they? Who are they ever?* I desperately wanted to ask, but her voice faded out. The line went dead.

I cried for days. This was long ago. Nothing so vivid has supplanted that dream. Some mornings, I wake to tears, but can't recall their cause, only a vague sense of something, someone, lost, a hurt the merciless world will visit upon us all in turn. It's common, though most don't speak of it, how walls built in waking hours can fall in an instant of fluttering hands. All of those delicate barricades downed.

Vanishing Structures

The old barn tilts sharp to the right. All of the windows were taken or broken long ago—boys with their bb guns and the quick thrill as each metal pellet cracked the fragile glass. An owl often occupies the oval window near the barn's peak—an oculus looking out across the prairie. Feral cats used to fill the barn each spring, giving birth to their litters in soft nests of rotting hay, but once the owl moved in, the cats scattered. Strong winds rock the structure year-round. It won't take much to bend the barn into the ground, just one more thunderstorm, or a blizzard, the heavy snow a weight no longer possible to resist.

A Bachelor Farmer and His Brother

They lived a couple of miles away, down a little-traveled gravel road just off the highway. My father knew Carl, the bachelor farmer, but no one knew his brother, a man who stayed in, people said, though no one knew why. People liked to keep to themselves. Like every man in that part of the country, Carl was reticent. His face was ageless, not old, not young, always blank. He was inscrutable. In the autumn, our father would take us to visit, and Carl would let us collect fallen chestnuts. His yard was filled with those trees. I was dazzled by the smooth, shiny brown nuts to be found inside their spiny, off-putting outer hulls. I was around eleven years old the last time I saw him. Our father disappeared after that. I don't know what became of Carl. No one knew what happened to his brother. Like all farmers, his bones were made of soil. He aged and faded back into the land that had birthed him.

Portrait of My Sister

She stands in the cemetery, windblown, a baby on one hip and a jug of water on the other. The wall of tall pines at the front of the graveyard do little to shield her from the late May sun. We've come to tend our sister's grave. We know something of death. There's a small bronze vase that comes up out of the otherwise flat plaque affixed to the flat headstone. In spring and summer, we try to keep it filled with flowers, though the flowers last only a few days, and if the sun is bright and high, even less. When I look at her, I see myself, each shared feature slightly recast, too similar to mistake.

Smith's Mill

Burn (I)

We inhabit the houses we live in, and they, as much, inhabit us. I have a photograph of a large, gray door. It came from the house I grew up in, though I can't say in which threshold it belonged, or how it came to rest, finally, against the old picnic table in the back yard. I don't know what happened to it. Weathered by years of winters and summers, warped, rotted, my mother probably burned it in the large wire fire pit she built in the middle of the half-acre where we used to grow all the potatoes we'd need for a winter. Eventually, everything ended up there. She had no taste for the past. Nostalgia, too cloying a scent. When she finally left that house, after nearly fifty years, she ended up in the place she now owns—her little old lady house. The old house burned down a few years ago. Bad wiring or arson. No one could say. The new owners built a sprawling ranch style over the pit where our old house sank. Fire takes everything. It's an efficient way to erase our lives, make space for the new things we'll one day long to be rid of.

Burn (II)

My grandfather was a pyromaniac. He saw fire as a way to cleanse the world of all the junk that filled it. He grew up poor in Northern Italy, lived in a house inhabited only by what was necessary. When something broke and couldn't be fixed, you burned it. A small mound of ashes takes up so much less room than a boxful of broken bowls or an abandoned car. Grandfather lived with us when I was a child, and though we were poor, we still managed to collect things. This was a different age, filled with disposable materials. In the country there is no curbside garbage service, so as things broke, as trash cans filled, it all ended up in a pile back behind the house. Maybe it was more than a pile. Maybe it was a hill, or even a mountain in our flat terrain. Grandfather couldn't stand it. It seemed perfectly normal to me. His solution was simple: burn it. Let the trash mountain crumble in upon itself, turn to ash, then scatter the ash in the garden. But there was so much of it. He underestimated how far the flames would leap. It nearly burned the house down, and my family had to fight the fire for hours. My grandfather didn't understand why my mother was so angry with him, but several weeks later she loaded him into the car and drove him home to Nebraska. I never saw him again. My mother has acquired her own love of fire and every day, consigns more of our past to the flames. My family has taken to the cremation of our dead, but I don't like to get too close to any open flame.

Jeanette (Sitting In The Living Room With My Sister, Who Is Dying)

So familiar, the wet, drowning cough, the breath's rasp, like heavy
sandpaper on wood. We've been here before. Another sister, another
city, twenty-five years ago. Now the first sister has been dead for as
many years as she was alive. Her voice still lives inside my ear. And
so Jeanette, with her own note of unwilling passing. She reclines
on the couch and we watch television. It doesn't matter what's
on, only that something is there to fill the void between our two
worlds. Twice a month, she makes an eight-hour bus trip from
Sioux Falls to Saint Paul to take an experimental drug that could
save her life. She says she'd risk anything for that, even the possible
side effects of hair loss, or, the growth of hair all over her body.
It's a new drug, an inexact science. We joke about werewolves and
electrolysis, but know she's serious. Any cost for life. At sixty-one
she's ancient in the cystic fibrosis world. Linda died at thirty. The
doctors then considered her old. I feed Jeanette rich foods to fatten
her up, homemade ice cream, protein bars, anything to add some
weight. On a windy day like today, when autumn is carrying summer
away, I fear she could lift on a draft and fly all the way to the next
world. How far is that? So I tether her with heavy blankets and
heavy food. She wants, she says, to have her own apartment one
day, away from her daughter and grandchildren, their noisy lives.
I pray she lives that long, for the day when all that she can see will
be her own.

New Hampshire Girl, 11, Vanishes

It couldn't literally happen like that, but language is imprecise, so the girl disappears in a flash, the way a magician's assistant disappears, then reappears, on the other side of the auditorium. Or the girl disappears under supernatural circumstances, vanishes in real time before our very eyes, out of this dimension. Because energy never ceases to exist, she must be someplace, another world, an alternate plane, a space which we don't yet understand. The New Hampshire girl's family lives in willful disbelief. Despite what the police say, they won't give up. Why should they? Isn't hope better than knowledge?

My sister was selected from the audience by a famous illusionist for a part in his act. He caused her to vanish from one box and brought her back in another. He made her promise never to reveal the secrets of his trick. So far, she has not. One day, she'll disappear again, and we'll know, despite our grief, that she'll never return. They never do. She won't give up her secret, but we'll refuse that silence, go on looking.

Séance (Ghost Story II)

If there was a way to talk with you, I don't think I'd use it. Titillating, the notion of communicating with another plane, my voice finding your voice in a vague celestial space between one world and another. But frightening. The gift the dead give us: silence. We claim we have things to say, apologies to make; we know it can never be, so we talk big. One evening, by myself, I saw a pale white form on the stairs. It was a woman. She seemed utterly alone. Not at peace. Not in torment. Dispossessed of the earth. I was terrified. Better to speculate on the next world. Ghosts taunt us with all we don't know. So stay quiet my dear, please. Let me forget the shape of your face. Allow me to lose, through time and attrition, your voice's timbre.

RIVER FLATS

The Mississippi runs broad and deep in this part of the city. The flats stretch from the shore to the cliffs that edge the river gorge. No one visits this city park, full of sand and scrub willow and weeds. There are no visible paths. But night flowers do bloom in the warmer months, as the men roam the sandy loam in the dark. Their feet know where to go. One mouth meets another the way thirsty lips meet water, and the sound of the rushing river drowns out all of those pleasured cries. Thorny gooseberry thrives here. Poison ivy and poison oak. Some would call this land contaminated. Others, a paradise.

WINTER VIGNETTE, MINNEAPOLIS, 1987

I ride with Tom in his 1960 Nash Metropolitan over the ice-covered Minneapolis streets in the dead of winter — late January — in sub-zero temperatures in the middle of a massive blizzard in a car that doesn't belong in this place or time. The windows are frozen over because the little car's heater cannot compete with the cold's constant onslaught. I roll down my window to try and scrape the windshield on the outside and my arm and face are blasted numb. The poor car's bald tires cannot grip the road so we skate across the ice-covered streets, laughing hysterically because there's nothing else to do, but abandon the tiny car on the street; laughing hysterically because we choose to live here, in this arctic misery, and we like it; laughing hysterically because this car is a misfit in this climate, because we are misfits in this world; laughing hysterically because everything here is inconvenient and the entire city is lost to the cold.

A Former Home for Wayward Girls

We lived, then, in a house he bought for cheap in a downwardly mobile neighborhood. It had once been an opulent mansion, then a Catholic home for wayward girls. When we first arrived, we found used syringes hidden under the carpet all over the basement, and thick steel safety doors at the foot and head of each staircase. My bedroom was occupied by the ghost of an angry nun. Every night, as I tried to sleep, she kicked the underside of the mattress. Some nights, she violently shook the bed. She must have been outraged that two gay men and a lesbian had moved into her house, and were slowly pulling the whole place apart, room by room, and restoring it. At first, I was frightened, but after months of sleeplessness, I was just angry. Using silent prayers, I wished her away. First, out of the room. Then, out of the house. Then, out of the yard. And finally, into the stars, where she belonged. I felt her leave the night her soul was finally pulled up by heaven's holy vacuum. Suddenly, I could breathe. For the first time since we'd moved in, I slept through the night.

On the Invention of the Moving Image

In *La Jetee*, Chris Marker's film constructed primarily of still photographs, there's a moment of movement toward movie's end, when the time traveler and the woman from the past, whom he's come to love, are in bed, and the woman turns, slowly. We hear a bit of breath, a sheet brushing against skin. We see a lock of her hair falling gently over her face.

I have a video of him, filmed accidentally when I thought I was taking his photo. He sits, nonchalantly, on the bed, in the background the sound of birdsong and traffic. He barely moves, just turns his head toward the camera, then away. It's over in seconds. It betrays nothing of the days ahead. I've played it every day since he passed. A small prayer.

THE LOVER

In an ordinary house in a lower-middle class neighborhood, in its dank basement, where most of the light bulbs were blown and the coin-operated washer and dryer sat, there was a room that looked like someone once lived there: an old wooden table, an empty bed frame, a single chair. We couldn't imagine who would stay in such a place; someone who likely died from the mold that infested every corner of the room. Our apartment, two floors up, was dry but drafty. I wasn't the first to experience the visitations. My room-mates had their stories first. Mine was simple: some nights, while falling asleep, I felt hands pressing down the blankets on either side of my body, starting at my feet, running up to my shoulders. Then, a weight on top of me, an invisible man lying down with his unwitting lover. I never felt threatened. I understood the spirit, lonely, trapped in a desperate cycle. I knew something about that.

Life Among Men

Like the Dog Star, the one astronomers say is there but we cannot
see it. Like a sly ghost, existing only in the corner of the eye. Like
that, the truth behind all men's eyes, that wariness, that hunger,
smirking mouth, the lips wet with kissing, with devouring.

Stray errata on the Internet. A simple search with related terms and
you might come up with anything. You might come up with him, a
dozen photos (here they're *pics*) of bodies in motion. Which is his?
Which hand? Which chest? The pattern of hair there between each
nipple a map you must surely recognize. Stray erotica on the Internet.
Here, everyone's a headless star or, like a photographer friend of
mine once proved, every man is a shirtless star, a red ball cap obscures
his face. My friend found these men using simple search terms: *sex
+ ball caps + men*, then spliced them together into an endless red
capped loop, Andy Warhol's dream of an infinitely reproducible
sex machine.

The rest have our secrets. Light behind the eyes that says some-
one's home, hoarding knowledge of the world that would make
your head spin. Really. Too pretty to be alive so he must be up
to something. Too plain to rate the slightest stare so he can't be
up to anything. Too run-of-the-mill so you cannot care what he's
thinking. The ordinary know the extraordinary won't show us the
slightest attention, so we can do as we please among ourselves,
invisible as Dog Stars. We can get away with anything.

Flood

Syringes and refrigerators, tires and pans, heavy engines, and a man, or, his body, wrapped up in a beautiful blue tarp. Pop bottles, prescription bottles, pensioner minus her pension check, barkalounger, lingerie twisted into broken oak branches. Clouds of cottonwood fluff congealed with river foam, a radiator, wheel barrow, aged radical from the '60s. Plaster statues, faces green with moss, faces worn smooth by the water's hands. Hats and rabbits, missing magician's assistant, stage prop, lollipop with the tongue print of the child who last licked it. Bicycles minus tires, boys without feet, girls with hair like haloes spreading out in the water, weathered crosses, basket of beets, prayer beads, horns of the Devil, hands of God, bucket and mop, rolling pin. Two pounds of tomatoes, a pointed stick, coil of rope, crate of chickens, corn on the cob, baseball bat, and severed head, eyes open, a smile on the pale lips. Careless love, careful love, no love, all love caught up in a grappling hook. Those who save themselves for marriage but never marry. Those who throw themselves into the viral pool and never float back up. Those rotten with longing, those rotten with desire, all of the satisfied and all of the starving, caught up in the river's constant going toward someplace always south of here.

SUPERIOR, LATE AUTUMN

Under the waves, a silent world undulates in the invisible current.
The fish are voiceless. Above the waterline, the constant thrash of
the tide against a rocky shore. Water batters broken basalt, carries
it back into the sea, bit by bit. What if the world above fell quiet?
Silent waves. The wind, whipping craggy pines, bending them to
its will, but soundless? The birds overhead, we'd only know them
by their circling shadows, an occasional feather drifting downward.

Heliotrope or hydrangea. Anemone. Night-blooming cereus. Some delicate white flower that lasts a single day or night. Crystal or cell, each snowflake unique, gives up that life for the communal, the yard covered in feet of snow, or a winter cave carved in unstable drifts.

Bright sun. Dazzling sun. The blindness of a morning's commute or an afternoon's errand. The angle of the sun, as it rises or sets, directly in your eyes.

Slow sleep. Drifting into numbness, then the sensation of heat, the urge to undress, roll away into the arms of the snow.

Amnesia. All that we forget about winter just before the first storm, just after the last.

Hibernation. Eating sweets. Craving fats. Insulation and deep beds, thick pillows, burrowing down under heavy blankets. Curled sleepers, like the animals that know how to escape the cold, like the animals that should, but cannot.

Saint Paul

The city wasn't large, though it wasn't small. Large enough to get lost in; small enough to almost guarantee a safe return home. In the dark months, it wrapped itself in mystery: unlighted, unnumbered doorways; cobblestone streets winding around old grain mills; abandoned houses; small, seldom-used parks. The man liked to walk at night, when the weather permitted, and look for things. He never knew what he sought until he found it. Once, a stuffed bobcat, patchy fur, broken fangs; once, a tooth that seemed to have been pulled fresh from someone's mouth; once, a grandfather clock, towering, faceless.

He filled his home with the things he found, believing what was discovered was meant to be, was given into his care by some guiding force. Who was he to say no to the universe? He started on the garage once the house filled, started on the yard when the garage filled. But the elements can be harsh on fragile treasures. Winter came. He woke to find his yard erased, each distinct shape now a vague white form. Some details remained: strait-back chair he found at a stoplight; small marble hand broken from a monument in a graveyard. As dawn opened on the worst of winter's artistry, he saw the hand beckoning, a cold premonition.

ALICE

Do you remember Alice, running up the staircase in dawn's pale light? Asleep at the window, a slight summer wind gently lifting her hair? Do you know how often I look for her when I enter any room in this house, or pass through memory's rooms in the house before this one? She is bound up in the land around me. In the paper birch. In the lilac. In the sidewalk. In the tarmac. In the hill we live on, that gently slopes down to the wide Mississippi. She is bound up in this city. In the rough cobblestone drives. In the meandering streets that follow no logical grid, in every nineteenth century building, in every one of the grand Victorian houses that line Summit Avenue. She is bound up in my body's cells, buried that deep. How could I forget her, living, as she does, in my fingertips, on the surface of everything I touch?

On Sundays

All of the gray skies in the world won't equal the gray skies of this day. Unmake the guest bed, then make it again. Put away the clothes that have sat in piles for weeks.

She tells me our mother won't hear what the doctors say and she sounds cancerous with anger. How is it that love can be sewn into the leaves of hatred, bound up between the same covers? Death, if not by choice, is not abandonment, but we'll cry at the injustice nonetheless.

Clear away the dishes, run the vacuum over the rug and pray for accidents that bring good fortune instead of bad.

In Tongues

My words had grown impossible so I stitched my mouth shut. The little sparrows inside beat their wings frantically, trying to escape. None wanted to live in that wet black confine, listening to the stunted mumblings of a man who'd rendered himself speechless. Poor captive audience. Each folded its wings and slipped, resolute, into the throat of silence.

My tongue had grown flaccid. The language I'd learned as a child was gone. What isn't practiced is lost, unreachable except by miracle or injury. Once a man was struck on the head and woke to find he spoke fluent German, but had lost his native tongue. Undone in his own country, a stranger to his family, he flew away. A thousand sparrows formed a feathered carpet and carried him off to Germany. A stranger to everyone, he stopped up his mouth with a thousand sparrows. Each spring he sang in notes he couldn't recognize.

My hands have become impossible. They're signing all day long. I don't know what they're saying, so it's better to be here, where everything is spoken and no one is punished. My fingers take flight, spell a thousand sparrows back into the sky. The bell is ringing; it's time for you to go. You can exit out the terrace doors, cut across the lawn. No one will mind. I don't know what my fingers speak. Forgive me if I don't wave back.

The Internet Can't Save You

The Internet can't save you. Your smart phone won't make you smart. A thousand likes doesn't mean anyone likes you. Constant connection isn't constant connection if that connection comes from invisible bits of data flying through the air at impossible speeds. Invisible data can't kiss you. It cannot hold you if you need to be held. It won't love you. A twenty-four hour newsfeed won't feed you, won't sustain you. Reading online about starvation won't save you from starvation. You can't eat a terabyte and it won't fill your belly. Face Time isn't face-to-face time. The World Wide Web is a web, a spider's trap. The Internet is not a net, won't catch you if you fall. Your iPhone isn't a lifeline. It's not an oxygen line. It's not even a telephone line. A cell tower ping doesn't place you anywhere. A cell tower ping isn't proof of your existence. One website or a million websites, there is no *there* there. There is no where there. An avatar is a poor proxy for reality. Your Instagram presence is less than a thread of smoke drifting on the wind. Your body isn't digital. Your skin holds your body inside of something. It's more than a shell, less than a prison. The Internet can't save you. Nostalgia's a trap. You can't remember when if something happened a second ago. You don't live in a cloud. You can't store anything in a cloud. A cloud is nothing but vapor. A heavy gust and everything's gone. Memory is more than data. The Internet can't save you. Virtual reality isn't real at all. Connectivity does not equal connection. A tweet isn't a conversation. A tweet often isn't even a sentence, though a tweet can result in one. Online doesn't equal awakened or aware. An emoji isn't an emotion, doesn't stand in for an emotion, cannot replace an emotion. There is no life in your digital life. Your vision is broader than any screen. Your life does not fit on a microchip. A million selfies do not equal a self, do not mean you know yourself. A million followers does not mean anyone follows you, knows you, wants to be by your side. Your personal profile is not personal. A troll is a creature that lives under a bridge. A catfish is a creature that swims in muddy rivers. The Internet won't save you. An app does not apply. A million hits is not a million caresses, is not a single moment of skin-to-skin, is not a touch, is not a tap, is not a stroke, not a strike. There is no second life on the Internet. There was never a first.

In the Old House

A stark light falls through the kitchen, carrying an image with it:
the shadow of an old woman. It happens just that fast, a flash. I
blink and she's there. I blink. She's gone.

All that I know of myself—my looks, my moods—come from her.
I've seen myself in her eyes, her face in mine. She's never entered
this house, the place I call home.

I feel her staring through plaster and lathe. The sound of her voice,
the scent of her body, fill each room.

One day, I was dreaming she was gone and woke and found that
really, she was gone. Then, I wanted nothing more than to find her,
raise her up, bring her back.

Part of the Way Home

I've meant, for many months, to get there. The road isn't long, the route, not too crooked. I've been in the car, hands on the wheel, moving down the street. Somehow, I get lost. I always get lost. I've checked the lunar calendar, consulted the star charts, to determine the most auspicious days for travel. I've noted landmarks by which I'll navigate: the odd church with half a steeple; the truck stop with the fiberglass cow atop a one hundred foot pole. I mean well. I know she won't last. If I could tell her why I hesitate, I'd be free to travel any road. I can see the green glider in front of the garage, the square bed of vivid red poppies. My mother, who has always had to be too patient, waits in the armchair. The television's on too loud, and she's going deaf. She won't hear the phone when I call again to say I won't be driving down after all.

SEVEN WONDERS

A resolute man, in his hunger for wonder, goes searching for the next best thing. The original Seven Wonders are obsolete. Their time is done. Each is taken apart, brick by brick by log by stone. Enough is left so that the man might be punished when he sees what's become of them. He travels for years and thinks he finds new wonders. His suitcase expands and contracts as he adds, then subtracts those things he thought were rarities. Time passes and winds blow and finally, everything is buried in sand. What's left in museum collections won't thrive. Marble faces on proper British walls grow sad and sag until they're expressionless. No one remembers what the great Sphinx said and the Hanging Gardens are gone, like the Colossus of Rhodes, ghosts in their own lands. The resolute man never returns home. Hunger knows no bounds and what might have been his garden paradise is now a desert. Who would recognize him? His name fades from history and his portrait, made when he was young, resembles no one, or anyone: pale green eyes, short brown hair, a smile shy, but beguiling.

Dream Garden

Just as flamingos acquire their pink color by consuming brine shrimp, I want to stand in a school of glittering fish until my skin turns iridescent, rainbow-hued. I want to wash away the white a lack of sun has caused, the paleness of hours in dark libraries, of days spent in front of the computer's cold blue screen. I want the shimmer of glitter, an inexhaustible shift from one color to another. I want my body to mimic mother-of-pearl, abalone, and opal, nightglowing, synthesizing light, breathing out beautiful oxygen. I want to grow scales, grow feathers, camouflage myself in startling pigments. I want to take my gorgeous body into the trees and sing, unfold a tail tall and blue and covered in one hundred startling eyes. I want to lie on the emerald grass and see my skin turn emerald green, or pose among the slender Siberian irises and shine out a brighter shade of purple. I want to jump into a spring and turn crystalline, brown, black and tan, the color of the water and the smooth-worn rocks at the bottom of the stream's bed. I want to turn verdant green, like the moss along the shore. I want to become lost in a sea of sunflowers, my beautiful black and yellow face turned, like the rest, toward the nourishing sun.

Nightmare (*The Phantom Carriage*)

New Year's Eve, twenty minutes to twelve, and the night is cold and blue, and the sky is stumbleful of stars. Three drunken friends stand on a street in a northern city. They're freezing. They stamp their numb feet. One tells a ghost story. As he speaks, cigarette smoke mingles with his frozen breath. The story says that he who dies last before the New Year begins is condemned to drive Death's carriage.

Grief is a night-blooming flower. A wealthy man sits in his well-appointed office. He looks out over a city bright with celebration. The old year is about to turn. The planet spins. Without looking down, he takes a pistol from a drawer. It's a well-practiced move. Letters to his loved ones are scattered across the floor. He places the pistol barrel in his mouth and pulls the trigger. The flower blooms.

A solitary man thrashes in the bay's frigid water. Rough waves kick hard against the stony shore. Seaweed wavers around him, and his body dances in time. Finally exhausted, he no longer struggles. The blue night wraps him tightly, and the moon's light bends crooked through the water's lens.

Alcohol makes them mean, and the drunken friends fight. Every punch is bitter. Each is covered in bruises and blood. One dies just before midnight, before the second hand stretches into the New Year. The carriage arrives. It's bright as the moon. There's always room for one more. He mounts the seat and takes the reins.

In the unexpected heat of a late autumn day, I speak aloud all of those things I no longer want. I call them out by their names. They can't hide in the sharp October light. They can't be buried under brittle brown leaves. I say their names and they appear, one by one. They look at me. Then, they disappear.

Everything smells so ripe and dry. Dead leaves skitter along the street. Listless bees move from flower to flower, but there's nothing left to eat. My body wants to pull itself apart, my limbs want to scatter themselves among the weeds and wild asters. Twenty years ago, I didn't know what a wild aster was, or why autumn always brought me to my knees in breathless fear. Now I know why these things occur, and I say, everything that has the will to bloom is a flower.

Wrens at the feeder in early November. A single white cosmos blooms atop its spindly stem. Blood red lily stalks are dry and brown, their leaves, long blades. Some boys are going door to door, offering to rake or bag leaves for cash. Everywhere, houses in foreclosure. The inhabitants abandon their lives. The neighborhood fills with strays. A black cat approaches, sweet and small. I give him some food and water. He finishes it, then quietly moves on.

THANKSGIVING EVENING

The sky, struck white by a curtain of cloud, and the fields, in their blanket of snow, collide at the horizon. The swell of the land disappears in this uniformity of pale gray light. The meadow, a dip between slight hills, resembles a frozen lake. The landscape is unrecognizable.

This afternoon my mother joked about seeing the bright white light before Christmas. She's ninety-four, and has earned the right to joke about dying. It's not so easy for me, as I reconcile the world with and without her in it.

Just before dusk, the sun breaks through the cloud's curtain. It's the golden hour. The leaves that still cling to the gnarled oaks glow beautifully. The fields of dull, close-cropped stalks shine. At such times, we are all lovely.

Abandoned Asylum

asy·lum noun \ə-'sī-ləm
: a hospital where people who are mentally ill are cared for especially for long
periods of time : a mental hospital

They believed beauty had the power to soothe an unquiet mind, and so built brick castles on hilltops, in forests, any location with an exquisite view, but far enough removed for the comfort of the people in neighboring towns.

: an inviolable place of refuge and protection giving shelter to criminals and
debtors : sanctuary

See the way the tongue-in-groove wood has been soaked, then slowly bent, to fit the gentle curve of the rounding hallway ceiling?

: a place of retreat and security : shelter

See the staircases that ascend, grand and wide, to the upper floors, to the dormitories segregated by sex. Evidence of the sure hands of master carpenters, who spun the delicate balustrades from single blocks of wood. This roof is strong.

a : the protection or inviolability afforded by an asylum : refuge

See the yellow kitchen tile work, the blue bathrooms, the craftsmanship that demanded each small square be perfectly placed, evenly colored and glazed.

: an institution for the care of the destitute or sick and especially the insane

It seems like a restful dream, a haven from a world that will not accommodate difference. Beyond the perfection of the trim, carefully selected wallpapers, the usual horrors reside.

Origin of ASYLUM: Middle English, from Latin, from Greek asylon, neuter
of asylos inviolable, from a- + sylon right of seizure. First Known Use:
15th century

Ice water baths. Crude electro-shock. Straight jackets and strangle-holds. Finally, the lobotomy, sharp pick to sever that troublesome lobe in the brain where all our humanity sits. Above all things, unity of place, of mind. Tranquility under the garden arbor.

Related to ASYLUM

I wander the empty rooms and see my father's ghost. I see my own. They live together in the walls. They pass through windows and visit the fields beyond the fences, find their own numbered, nameless stones in the discrete graveyard behind the infirmary. Number one-nine-one-two. Number one-nine-six-three.

Synonyms: madhouse, bedlam, institution

No beauty in pharmaceuticals, no hand-carved woodwork or in-tricate plaster crown molding to bring about a precise mind. A handful of pills taken twice daily do not soothe so much as blunt.

Related Words: hospital; home; hospice, sanatorium, sanitarium, sanitorium

In abandoned palatial clinics, sheets obscure rotting furniture and the collapsing walls are covered in graffiti. Dry leaves and torn records tumble down the gently curing corridors. All of the lives engrained in the woodwork, play themselves over and over again. A broken record. A broken record. A broken record.

Occupation

Those times when hours pass and I forget to breathe are less common.
Now, too often pallid, stuttering.

        Flow: as in river.

               Flow: as in blood.

But slower. Rapids turn to rivers, rivers to streams. How often do I
work, thirsty? My mouth is always dry, my tongue stuck to its roof.
Language grows desperate. Younger bodies are supple. They ripple
across rooms and pages. I touch them as I touch the tide, tentatively.
They're always in motion, confident in the journey. I travel now less
frequently, and haltingly, but the world's still beautiful in its speed.

CYANOTYPE

Blue, the color of my heart. Blue upon blue upon blue. Blue trees with blue leaves. Blue hills and blue grass. Blue wind and blue snow. Blue heart. Blue woman in blue dress. Blue man in blue suit. Blue sky with blue clouds. Blue children on the blue playground. Blue lake and blue shore. Blue sandcastles and blue gulls and blue cattails at the lake's swampy blue edge. Blue eyes and blue skin. Blue horses rearing. Blue dogs barking. Blue cats sleeping in the warm blue sun. Blue highway and blue cars. Blue drivers going to blue homes or blue office buildings or blue shopping malls. Blue graveyard and blue headstones. Blue names and blue dates. Blue spruce and blue pine. They form a blue wall around a blue house. We, who are blue, live our blue lives inside it, but we are invisible, disappearing, as we do, into the blue walls of every room.

The pandemic reduces my world to what can be found within the walls of my house. A little over thirteen hundred square feet. In despair I turn to cat rescue videos online. My new landscape is shaped by Facebook, with old vacation photos my friends post, *name that artist, author, singer, composer* challenges, and animal rescue videos. The world is filled with so much hurt that I can't stand to watch the news. What can anyone do with tragedy piled on tragedy, but sink under that weight, and give up? It's a privilege to be able to give up. Many don't have that choice. The world rests more heavily on their shoulders. They persevere because they must.

I watch the cat rescue videos because they guarantee a happy ending. No one posts those stories where the kitten doesn't make it, though I know those tales are more common than not. Their plots are all a variation on *The Little Princess.* Suffering, tribulation, and near catastrophe, and then, a savior. Some kindly human. The little lost things always find their forever homes and I shed tears of relief.

No so in the world outside these carefully edited scenes. Here, black men are shot for walking down the street, and buildings burn because rage and injustice can no longer be stifled. Our nation sits nervous on the edge of fascism, and every night, curfews are called. We run into our houses, if they still stand, at eight o'clock and lock the doors. Neighbors don't always wave now when they see neighbors passing on the sidewalk. The air itself is suspect. For many nights, I can smell smoke from the fires consuming the street front stores, the small restaurants that will never reopen. Whenever I leave my house, I must wear a mask, because my breath might kill someone, and anyone else's breath could kill me.

I spend days in my tiny office, a room at the back of my little house. Through the single window the only things I see are my backyard, the two stray brother cats who live in my garage. Their story is slightly happy, but I cannot take them in. I've grown to love them over the years we've spent in proximity to one another. I see them. They see me. They know I'll protect them as best I can, and I know they are unlikely to abandon me. Sometimes, proximity has to be enough.

Summer Garden *(Dream)*

Sometimes, life is a blessing. When the balloon flowers bloom and open up their blue cups to the rain. In the wildflower patch, where as many weeds as flowers grow, there is a certain joy in that green chaos, when unexpected reds and yellows and pinks show their faces amidst the lush thicket of leaves. She once thought of herself as a flower, but that was decades ago. Most plants will bloom if you leave them alone, even here, in the featureless flatness of endless fields of soybean and corn. The rhubarb will send up tall, hollow stalks with a froth of white at the top. Asparagus will send out slender branches and every branch will bloom until the plant resembles a miniature tree. Just once, she'd like to see a different crop in the fields that wall in the dwindling town. A field of poppies, or a field of sunflowers. She can't remember when her life lost its color. She's not sure why she's still alive. But autumn comes, inevitably, and when it does, she'll put the flowerbeds to sleep, and disappear, at last, into all of that dark quiet.

The Cemetery on the Hill

Amidst such flatness, there are swells here and there, as if the ground's belly heaved up in laughter or sorrow and made hills, some so subtle you'll never see them. On the hill in our tiny town, the graveyard sprawls out across the rise. If you're driving by on the re-routed freeway, you can see it there. Only the dead have this view: a lovely valley, another hill swelling up on the other side. This isn't *Our Town*, so no dead sit on chairs near their graves and offer commentary on the lives of those they've left behind. This is just a cemetery. This is where the dead go when they've run out of things to say, when their bodies are broken beyond repair. My father lies here. My sister. Now, my mother. When I visit their graves to leave the live flowers the groundskeeper will throw away the minute I'm gone, I listen. It's always so quiet, except for the wind, which never seems to stop whispering through the tongues of the leaves and grasses. I try to hear what the dead have to tell me. I hunger for their wisdom. But they offer only silence. Perhaps, if I had a gift for such things, I could hear them or see them, and they would have a world of knowledge to share. But I lost that ability when I was a child, like most do. So, I hear nothing. But silence, too, is a kind of message.

At Last

Did you look for me in all of the usual places? Out walking along the deserted gravel road? Out among the trees in the moonlight, my shadow melded to their tall, thick trunks? Did you think it was me when you saw the glowing eyes of the nocturnal animals staring out at you from the tall grass? Did you look for me in those places where you wanted most to find me? The bedroom. The kitchen. The wide front porch, sitting on the old swing's crumbling seat? Or did you look for me in those places I love most? The library, late at night, drifting like dust among the well packed stacks? The old movie house that plays a different pair of classic films every night? Or the used bookshop? Or the great glass conservatory, hiding among the orchids and the palms, my face a mask of flowers? Did you find me, or someone who looks like me? My face is unremarkable. My hair a common brown. My eyes green like the algae that blooms at the edges of a still pond. Did you find me or someone you wanted to be me? Hope shapes our vision. Desire warps it. If you can't see me, perhaps I'm only a spirit, what remains of a dream once the dreamer wakes. Or a ghost. Can you say what a ghost is? Can you tell me I am not one?

Acknowledgements

The poems listed below have appeared, sometimes in earlier versions, with other titles, in the following publications:

"Midwest Landscape: Unexplained Death"
"Midwest Landscape: Small Town Queers"
  Small Towns: An Anthology of Poetry
"Midwest Landscape: The First Man"
  Queer Voices
"Midwest Landscape: Abandoned House"
  The Wild Word (Haunted Issue)
"Midwest Landscape: Vanishing Structures"
"Midwest Landscape: Unexplained Death"
"Midwest Landscape: Long Gravel Drive"
  Watershed Review
"Midwest Landscape: Vanishing Structures"
  Sheila-Na-Gig
"Midwest Landscape: On Sundays"
"On the Invention of the Moving Image"
"Life Among Men"
  The Good Men Project
"Midwest Landscape: Empty Farm"
  The Outrider Review
"Flood" (as "In the Museum of Flotsam and Jetsam")
  Main Street Rag
"Seven Wonders"
  Whole Beast Rag
"Part of the Way Home"
  The Broad River Review
"New Hampshire Girl, 11, Vanishes"
  The Conium Review
"Midwest Landscape: Round Hay Bales"
  Sleet Magazine
"In Smith's Mill (Burn I, Burn II, Jeanette)"
  Nothing to Declare: A Guide to the Flash Sequence
"Ghost Story II (Séance)"
  Fogged Clarity

"Midwest Landscape: Poor" was first published under the title "Untitled Story (Poor)" in my collection, *Two Men Rowing Madly Toward Infinity* (Broadstone Books, 2016). It appears here in a revised version.

"Abandoned Asylum" (as "Asylum") was first published in my limited edition chapbook, *As Breath In Winter* (MIEL Press, 2015).

About the Author

William Reichard is a writer, editor, and educator. He has published seven previous volumes of poetry, including *The Night Horse: New and Selected Poems* (Brighthorse Books, 2018), and *Two Men Rowing Madly Toward Infinity* (Broadstone Books, 2016). Reichard is the editor of the anthology *American Tensions: Literature of Identity and the Search for Social Justice* (New Village Press, 2011), and he edited and revised the late Ricardo Brown's memoir, *The Evening Crowd at Kirmser's: A Gay Life in the 1940's* (University of Minnesota Press, 2001). He has received grants and awards from the Jerome Foundation, and the Minnesota State Arts Board.